PowerKiDS
Readers

Fun Fish

CLOWNFISH

Maddie Gibbs

PowerKiDS
press.

New York

Published in 2014 by The Rosen Publishing Group, Inc.
29 East 21st Street, New York, NY 10010

First Edition

Editor: Amelie von Zumbusch
Book Design: Andrew Povolny

Photo Credits: Cover Dan Exton/Shutterstock.com; p. 5 Levent Konuk/Shutterstock.com; p. 7 Hemera/Thinkstock; p. 9 Jodi Jacobson/E+/Getty Images; p. 11 Yusuke Okada/a.collectionRF/Getty Images; p. 13 formiktopus/Shutterstock.com; p. 15 cbpix/Shutterstock.com; p. 17 David Fleetham/Visuals Unlimited, Inc./Getty Images; p. 19 Reinhard Dirscherl/WaterFrame/Getty Images; p. 21 littlesam/Shutterstock.com; p. 23 Andaman/Shutterstock.com.

Library of Congress Cataloging-in-Publication Data

Gibbs, Maddie.
 Clownfish / by Maddie Gibbs. — First edition.
    pages cm. — (PowerKids readers: Fun fish)
 Includes index.
 ISBN 978-1-4777-0757-9 (library binding) — ISBN 978-1-4777-0847-7 (paperback) — ISBN 978-1-4777-0848-4 (6-pack)
 1. Anemone fishes—Juvenile literature. I. Title.
 QL638.P77G53 2014
 597'.72—dc23
                            2012045841

Manufactured in the United States of America

CPSIA Compliance Information: Batch #S13PK4: For Further Information contact Rosen Publishing, New York, New York at 1-800-237-9932

Contents

Clownfish are born male.

The biggest ones
become females!

A group is a **school**.

They live in oceans.

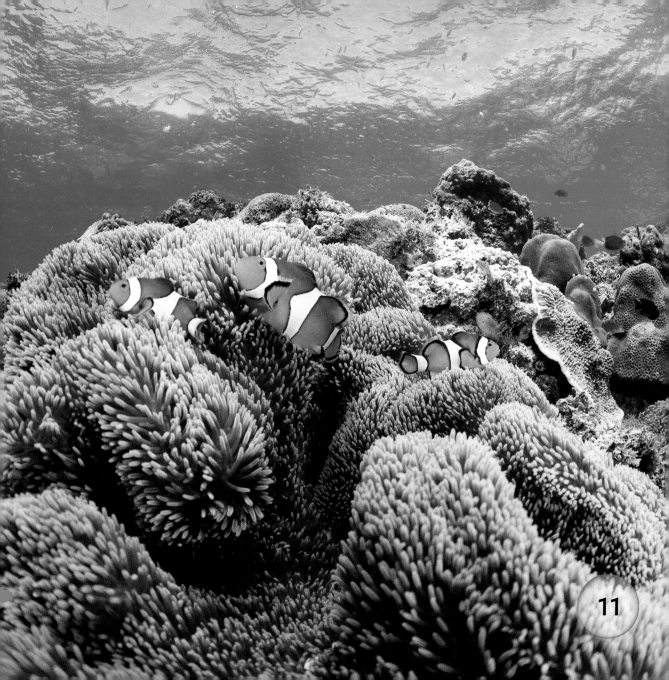

They live in **sea anemones**.
Anemones sting.

Goo covers clownfish.

It keeps them from being stung.

Fire clownfish can lay up to 500 eggs.

Ocellaris clownfish can live for 10 years.

Clownfish are cool!

WORDS TO KNOW

clownfish

school

sea anemone

INDEX

WEBSITES

Due to the changing nature of Internet links, PowerKids Press has developed an online list of websites related to the subject of this book. This site is updated regularly. Please use this link to access the list:
www.powerkidslinks.com/pkrff/clown/